Artists Through the Ages

Claude Monet

Alix Wood

WINDMILL BOOKS

New York

Published in 2013 by Windmill Books, An Imprint of Rosen Publishing
29 East 21st Street, New York, NY 10010

Editor for Alix Wood Books: Eloise Macgregor
US Editor: Sara Antill
Designer: Alix Wood

Photo Credits: Cover, 1 © Lefevre Fine Art Ltd., London / The Bridgeman Art Library
4 bottom right © Urban; 5 bottom © Mist - Fotolia; 6-7 © The Metropolitan Museum of Art;
8 © nga; 9 top © nga/ Chester Dale Collection; 9 bottom © nga; 11 © Blauel/Gnamm -
Artothek; 12 © Peter Willi - Artothek; 13 © Peter Willi - Artothek; 15 © rook76/shutterstock;
17 © The Metropolitan Museum of Art; 18 © Artothek; 21 © Christie's Images Ltd -
Artothek; 22 top © Christie's Images Ltd - Artothek; 22 bottom © Peter Willi - Artothek;
23 © The Metropolitan Museum of Art; 24-25 nga; 27 © nga/Chester Dale Collection;
28 © Christie's Images Ltd - Artothek; 3, 4 bottom left, 5 top, 14, 19, 20, 26, 29 © Shutterstock

Library of Congress Cataloging-in-Publication Data

Wood, Alix.
 Claude Monet / by Alix Wood.
    p. cm. — (Artists through the ages)
 Includes index.
 ISBN 978-1-61533-620-3 (library binding) — ISBN 978-1-61533-627-2 (pbk.) —
ISBN 978-1-61533-628-9 (6-pack)
 1. Monet, Claude, 1840–1926—Juvenile literature. 2. Painters—France—Biography—
Juvenile literature. I. Title.
 ND553.M7W66 2013
 759.4—dc23
 [B]

                                  2012025842

Manufactured in the United States of America

CPSIA Compliance Information: Batch #BW13WM: For Further Information contact Windmill Books, New York, New York at 1-866-478-0556

Contents

Who Was Monet?

Claude Monet was an **Impressionist** painter. He was born in Paris, the second son to his parents, Adolphe and Louise-Justine. His family moved to Le Havre when he was five. Monet's father was a partner in a ship supplies business. His mother was a singer. Monet loved to draw and paint even as a young boy.

Claude Monet

Map of the World

North America

Europe

Asia

Africa

South America

Australia

Le Havre

Paris

FRANCE

Today, Le Havre is a bustling port.

Monet didn't really like school. He drew funny pictures of his teachers. He got in trouble for his drawings, but they were very good!

He once said, "School seemed like a prison and I could never bear to stay there, especially when the sunshine beckoned and the sea was smooth."

Young Cartoonist

When Monet was only 11, he studied at the Le Havre school of the arts. He would sell charcoal **caricatures** of local important people for 10 to 20 **francs** each. When young Monet saved 2,000 francs from selling caricatures, he persuaded his father he could make a living from art.

Monet's Aunt

When Monet was 16, his mother died. Monet and his father didn't get along very well. Monet wanted to leave school without graduating. His father was not happy about this. Monet had an aunt, Marie-Jeanne Lecadre. She had no children of her own, and Monet went to live with her.

His aunt was an amateur painter. She let him use her **studio** and encouraged him. At about this time, he met fellow artist Eugène Boudin one day on the beach. Boudin became his **mentor** and persuaded Monet to stop drawing caricatures and to try oil paints instead.

The Garden at Sainte-Adresse, 1867. The garden in this painting is at his aunt's seaside villa. The people sitting down are thought to be Monet's father and his aunt.

Sky and Light

Monet spent two years learning to paint with Eugène Boudin. Boudin painted seascapes of Le Havre and liked to paint in the open air. Boudin thought that an artist should paint from his first impression of a scene. Monet's long career in art was then spent capturing these first impressions.

Boudin took Monet to paint with him outside. In Le Havre there is an amazing light, with rich, blue, cloud-filled skies. The Sun going in and out of the clouds made the landscape dark, then bright, in a flash. Monet and Boudin painted side by side, outside, using portable easels and paint in tubes, trying to catch the light.

Eugène Boudin

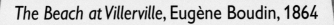

The Beach at Villerville, Eugène Boudin, 1864

Big Sky

Boudin often made the sky the main subject of his painting. Can you see his influence in Monet's style?

Sainte-Adresse, Claude Monet, 1867

Monet in Paris

Monet went to Paris in May 1859. His father expected him to go to the School of Fine Art. It was quite an old-fashioned art school. Monet's aunt gave him some money and he went to the Swiss Academy instead. It was cheaper and only had a few hours of classes a week, which suited Monet better.

Claude Monet as a young man

Monet made friends with other painters in Paris named Frédéric Bazille, Auguste Renoir, and Alfred Sisley. They called Monet a **"dandy"** because of the frilly shirts he wore. The friends had no money, and once lived on beans for two whole months!

Village Street in Normandy. Monet painted this around 1867. He and his friends liked to paint ordinary working people in clear, bright colors.

Talented Friends

The friends would paint together and exhibited at a new art gallery that took paintings the main art gallery had rejected. The painting below by Monet's friend Frédéric Bazille is of Bazille's studio and his friends. You can see the painters Auguste Renoir, Claude Monet, and Édouard Manet, the writer Émile Zola, and the musician Edmond Maître.

The Artist's Studio, Rue de la Condamine, Frédéric Bazille, 1870

1: Auguste Renoir

2: Émile Zola

3: Édouard Manet

4: Claude Monet

5: Frédéric Bazille

6: Edmond Maître

A Portrait

Louis-Joachim Gaudibert and his wife were a generous, wealthy couple who helped Monet in a bad year. His family had stopped sending him money. He had not sold any paintings and owed lots of money. He was thrown out of his house. The money he got for painting this portrait helped him carry on painting.

Madame Gaudibert, 1868

How Monet Painted

Monet only used a few colors when he painted. He never used browns and earth colors and, by 1886, he never used black either. Monet's paint **palette** would have looked like this. Some of the paints had different names then because they were made with things we now know are bad for you. For example, titanium white was made of lead then and called lead white.

french ultramarine

emerald green

cobalt blue

viridian green

alizarin crimson

cadmium yellow

vermilion

cadmium yellow light

titanium white

14

Monet liked to paint the way colors **reflected** in water. Monet even had a floating studio built for him, so he could float on the River Seine and paint. Monet kept paints, brushes, **canvas**, and drawing supplies on his boat.

Claude Monet in his Studio Boat, 1874, by Édouard Manet

Monet sometimes got in a bad mood when his paintings weren't going well. One day he threw all his paints and brushes in the river! The stamp above has a painting by his friend, Édouard Manet. It shows Monet in his studio boat with his wife, Camille.

A Time in the Army

Monet was selected for National Service and spent a year in North Africa in the army. He became ill with **dysentery** and his aunt managed to get him out of the army. His friend Bazille was not so lucky, and he was killed in 1870 fighting in a war.

In London

In July 1870 war broke out between France and Prussia, and Monet fled to London. He liked to paint the haze of **smog** that London had in that period. Monet liked to paint the Palace of Westminster, and did, more than a hundred times! He met the artists Charles-François Daubigny and Camille Pissarro while in London. He also met the art dealer Paul Durand-Ruel who sold his paintings for the rest of Monet's life.

Monet once said, "Durand-Ruel, became for us, our savior. For more than fifteen years, my painting as well as that of Renoir, Sisley, and Pissarro had no other market than through him."

The Houses of Parliament (Effect of Fog), 1903

Impressionism Is Born

In 1874 several painters including Monet, Renoir, and Pissarro held an exhibition of their work. Monet showed five paintings. This small painting below has become one of Monet's most important works, simply because of the title he chose, *Impression, Sunrise.*

Impression, Sunrise

An art critic said the painting looked "half-finished" like all the works on show, and he called the group "Impressionists." It was meant as an insult!

A Good Salesman

Monet sold his sunrise painting for 800 francs. After this, he often exhibited paintings with a sold sign already on them. This made his paintings seem very desirable and attracted more sales and higher prices.

SOLD

As his paintings began to sell, Monet could afford to take trips abroad. He went to Italy with his friend Renoir. The colors were so different in Italy, Monet had to start using a few new colors on his paint palette. He needed bright turqouise, pinks, and oranges. He once said "There are moments when I'm appalled at the colors I'm having to use."

Map Showing Italy and France

The House at Giverny

In 1870, Monet married Camille Doncieux. They lived with Ernest and Alice Hoschedé and their six children. Ernest had bought several of Monet's paintings in the past, but had now lost all his money. They moved to a large house in Giverny, in France. Monet loved to paint the house and the beautiful gardens he had made at Giverny.

A Full House

Monet, his wife Camille, and their two children, Jean and Michel, shared the house with Alice and Ernest Hoschedé and their children, Blanche, Germaine, Suzanne, Marthe, Jean-Pierre, and Jacques. Blanche later married Jean Monet. After Camille and Ernest had died, Monet married Alice.

A present-day photograph of Monet's house at Giverny

The Artist's House at Giverny, 1913

Monet spent many years designing the gardens at his new house. He built a water lily pond with a Japanese bridge over it. He had six gardeners who helped him with his designs. He planted lots of irises. They were his favorite flower.

Haystacks

Before Impressionism, an object was always painted the same basic color. Lemons were yellow and oranges were orange. Painting outdoors, rather than in a traditional studio, though, meant different light conditions at different times of the day.

Monet loved painting the changing light. He began painting haystacks at different times of day. He started with two canvases, but as the light changed, he asked his willing helper, his young step-daughter Blanche Hoschedé, to bring him more and more canvases in a wheelbarrow! Monet would rise before dawn and paint the first canvas for half an hour.

Haystacks, Morning Effect, 1891

Haystacks at the End of Summer, at Giverny, 1891

Haystacks (Effect of Snow and Sun), 1891

When the light changed, he would switch to the second canvas, and so on. The next day, he would do the same. In each painting, the color of the haystack is different because the light shining on the haystack is different.

Pulleys and Trenches

Monet loved painting outside. When he did a really large painting, he had a trench dug in the garden. That way, the canvas could be raised or lowered by pulleys to just the right height!

Monet's Garden

Monet now rarely left his garden to paint. He painted hundreds of views of his lily pond. The first paintings of the Japanese bridge at Giverny were quite conventional, like this painting on the right.

Later, Monet started experimenting. He did a series of paintings where his first canvas was painted from up high, looking down at the pond. Then Monet gradually moved down the bank until he was almost at eye level with the water. In the later paintings we can't tell if we are in the lake looking up or on the lake looking down. Filling the canvas, the surface of the pond becomes a world in itself.

The Japanese Footbridge, 1899

Rouen Cathedral

Monet spent three years painting the cathedral at Rouen, in France. He set up in a room with a window overlooking the cathedral. He would work on several canvases on the same day, like he did when he painted the haystacks. He would change canvases when the light changed. The cathedral would look misty blue, gray, or yellow depending on the weather and the light.

Changing Light

These two photographs are of the front of Rouen cathedral as it looks today. If you look at the trees in the background you can see they are taken at the same time of year—probably the same day—but the cathedral looks so different. Imagine if you started painting the top one and the light changed this much. You'd have to go back and start again!

Rouen Cathedral, West
Façade, Sunlight, 1894

Monet's Last Paintings

As Monet got older he began to lose his eyesight. **Cataracts** made his eyes see colors differently and made things blurry. Whites and greens now looked yellow, and reds became oranges. Blues and purples looked like reds and yellows to him. Monet went on painting, though. He knew what color he was using by the labels on the tubes and the order he put them on his palette.

The Japanese Bridge, around 1920

The painting on the left is of the same bridge as on page 25. It looks very different. It was done when Monet's eyes were at their worst. After a while the cataracts got so bad he was unable to paint. He had an operation which helped one eye to see.

Some of the last paintings Monet did were a series of enormous water lily murals. He built a special studio to paint them in. He had painted so many water lilies that he painted them from memory. Over 6 feet (1.8 m) high and up to 55 feet (16.75 m) long, they now hang in a museum in Paris called the Musée de l'Orangerie.

No Black for Monet

Monet died at the age of 86, at home in his bed. As Monet always avoided black in his painting, when he died his friend Georges Clemenceau didn't like the black sheet covering the coffin. He shouted, "No! No black for Monet!" and replaced it with a flowered cover.

The house and gardens at Giverny are now a museum.

Glossary

canvas (KAN-ves)
A piece of cloth used as a surface for painting.

caricatures
(KAR-ih-keh-churz)
Drawings that exaggerate a person's features for comic effect.

cataracts (KA-teh-rakts)
Clouding of the lens of the eyes.

dandy (DAN-dee)
A man who is very interested in his clothing and appearance.

dysentery (DIH-sun-ter-ee)
A painful illness of the intestine, with diarrhea, and often a fever.

francs (FRANKS)
The old unit of money of France and Belgium.

Impressionist
(im-PREH-shuh-nist)
An artist who concentrates on the impression of a scene using unmixed primary colors and small brush strokes to simulate light.

mentor (MEN-tor)
A wise and trusted
teacher.

palette (PA-lit)
A board used by a painter
to mix paints on.

reflected (rih-FLEKT-ed)
Light that is bent or
thrown back.

smog (SMOG)
A thick haze caused by
sunlight on air polluted
by smoke and fumes.

studio (STOO-dee-oh)
The working place of
an artist.

Websites

For web resources related to the
subject of this book, go to:
www.windmillbooks.com/weblinks
and select this book's title.

Read More

Connolly, Sean. *Claude Monet.* Lives of the Artists. New York: Gareth Stevens, 2005.

Monet, Claude, and The Metropolitan Museum of Art. *Monet's Impressions.* San Francisco, CA: Chronicle Books, 2010.

Waldron, Ann. *Who Was Claude Monet?.* New York: Grosset & Dunlap, 2010.

Index